Leaves
in October

Poems of Life, Love,
and Loss

Blessing on your journey, Beth

Beth Bricker Davis

For Mike

Cover Photo by David R. Edwards

"Dr. Mike" Photo by Chris McLean

Author Photo by Lenore Senior
fineartamerica.com/profiles/lenore-senior.html

ISBN-13:

978-1490376882

ISBN-10:
1490376887

Acknowledgments

With love and gratitude to –

My beautiful late parents, Clifford and Helen Bricker, who adopted me, nourished me, and loved me.

My incredible late husband, Dr. Mike Davis, who was, "The Best Husband in the Universe and Beyond," and who supported every facet of my creative life.

The publishers and editors of Pueblo Community College's art and literary journal, *The Final Note*, who have published some of my poems in each of their four volumes and steadfastly encouraged my writing.

Georgia Wynn (retired), Richmond High School, who taught me how to understand and properly use the English language, and Dr. Judith Roman Royer (retired), Indiana University, who first taught and encouraged my creative writing.

Marcia Beachy, MS, LPC, who read and appreciated much of my work and pushed me to, "Get it out there!"

Rev. Jude LaFollette, BCC, who read most of this book and served as an unofficial proofreader / editor, and official champion of my writing.

Many, many friends and family, who read and read and listened and listened to my poetry with open ears and loving hearts.

Raven Smith, for his kind formatting and publishing expertise, and Amy Zielinski, who capably served as the "official" editor of this book.

Preface

My husband of nearly 20 years, Mike, died suddenly in 2006, at the age of 54. A year after his death, I took a Creative Writing class at the college where Mike had been president, Pueblo Community College.

Taking the class was transformational. Being with college students, feeling energized by their youth, was just as healing as learning how to express my grief, and other ideas, through creative writing. My teacher, Jamie Bruss Patti, was enthusiastic and knowledgeable and was very supportive of my writing. It was a great ego boost during a time of huge transition and opened the flood gates of unexpressed feelings of grief at the sudden loss of my husband.

Since Mike's death, Mike's father, Paul; my mother, Helen; and my aunt and uncle, Mary and Clay, have also died. However, this is not simply a book of poems and stories about my grief. Some of the poems are sweet remembrances of loved ones and queries about what happens after death, like, "When

7

You Are Near." Other poems, like, "I Am From," are filled with gratitude for a joy-filled childhood. Some poems recognize the losses and love of others, like, "Luciana."

During my significant life transitions and throughout the creation of this book, my sweet, loyal, beautiful old dog, Nikki, has been at my side; this book would not be complete without a poem or two about the dog I adore.

I have included, "The Living Poem," in the preface to explain how some of the poems in this book were written or, more accurately, how they wrote themselves. My hope in sharing these poems and stories is that all of us who have been touched by loss and unexpected life transitions will find a sense of healing and be comforted by the commonality of our experiences.

The Living Poem

This poem forced me to
write it,
needling me in my sleep
on my comfortable,
restful Serta,
calling words and phrases
in my dreams,
like an aggressive director,
the poem was
shouting instructions,
waving its arms,
prying my eyes open
as soon as
I awakened,
pushing the notepad
with the attached Bic pen
on my nightstand
within arm's reach.

Finally, I succumbed,
rubbing my eyes,
adjusting my pillows,
sitting up in bed as slowly
as it would allow.

Pen to paper,
it wrote,
words tumbling over
the other,
jockeying for space,
high-spirited,
mis-spelled,
gleeful words,
released from their
slumber
and years of
quiet
containment.

Finally spent,
it collapsed
on itself,
panting,
wiping away tears,
mopping its brow,
quietly pulling
the white blue-lined paper over
its beautiful active verbs and
prepositional phrases.
Silent,
at last.

Table of Contents

Losing Mike

"Ever has it been that love knows not its own depth
until the hour of separation." Kahlil Gibran

Crossing "O"

Colorado sky,
once blue and clear
as an autumn day,
somersaulted in
ash gray and deep purple.

Cockpit instruments,
once bright as
lighthouse beacons,
flickered once,
then dimmed.
Forever.

One glance down
then straight ahead
to a perfect bull's eye
in the mountainside.

Spinning darkness,
rush of cold.
Faint glow down a
nameless funnel.
Quiet rushing of time
and space

and astronaut weightlessness.

Confusion and warmth and
warmth and confusion and
warmth and light and
light and love and
love and peace and
peace and love and
light and love.
And love and light.
And love and light.
And love.
And peace.
And light.

The Table

After Mike died, I spent a lot of time sitting at the new kitchen table. The grain in the oak was mysterious and inviting. The lines drew me in, drew me away. The padded faux black leather seats were soft and comfortable enough to offset the mission style chair, with its rigid, unyielding back slats. I was proud of my purchase.

I sat in Mike's spot at the head of the table. It was interesting to have a different perspective, and that way I didn't have to look at his empty space. I wondered what Mike would have thought of the table. It was a southwestern style. He would have liked that for sure. It was small enough for just four, but easily expanded to accommodate more for entertaining. He would have been happy that guests had a beautiful table at which to sit.

It was funny that we came from the Midwest with all our country-themed furniture and art work – the miniature milk jug filled with wooden spoons for the kitchen countertop; the wicker baskets and the hand-made wooden bins for potatoes – but were working so hard to assume this foreign decorative style. Mike liked change and was anxious to leave the old ways behind when we moved to Colorado. He would have been pleased that the new table was a mission style.

Before he died, Mike kept saying that we needed a new kitchen table. I would look at the old table and think, "What's the matter with it?" even though I could easily see the ground-in chocolate chip stains from Mike's Saturday morning baking rituals, and the black ink marks on the laminate tabletop from where we sat side by side on Sunday afternoons, paying bills and marking calendars for the week.

The first day at the furniture store was hard. I walked around and looked at each table - the long, cherry formal dining room table with two leaves and a faux brass planter of fake ivy; the square wrought iron table with ceramic tiles for a tabletop and high wrought iron bar stools for seats. As I approached each table, I missed Mike more. How could I choose a piece of furniture by myself for a life we built together? I missed Mike's input. I missed riding with him in the car to the store, my hand resting gently on his leg, laughing at "Car Talk" on the radio, or singing along to his Fleetwood Mac CD. I missed the sweet scent of his Burberry cologne and his musky Polo Deodorant. I missed walking hand in hand with him into the store like newlyweds. Mike probably would have chosen a table that first day. I did not.

As the weeks went by, I became more determined to find a new table – the *right* table. It was more than a table; it was a symbol. I can live alone. I can make decisions by myself. I can make a purchase for a life without Mike in it, but keep him in my heart.

When I found the table at an out-of-the-way furniture store, it screamed, "Mike." But more than that, it felt like, "us." In my mind, I could see us sitting together at the table in the store, stroking the beautiful oak tabletop, debating the price and discussing delivery options as the sales clerks escorted other couples through the store, winding their way through the oversized sofas and plush loveseats.

It was a bittersweet afternoon in March when they delivered and assembled the table. My dog, Nikki, and I watched patiently in the background while the men worked, quickly attaching the tabletop to its base and setting the chairs aright. After the men with their man-tools left, I sat quietly at the table, looking at Mike's photo staring back at me with his *Groundhog Day*-like forever smile and his ever-pressed light gray suit.

It was a moment of transition. It was a moment of remembering. It was a moment of strength and movement away from something known, to something unknown. The longer I sat at the table, the more I realized, it also said, "me."

Aspen Leaves in October

I hate this grief
but relish it and
roll in it
like a hound dog marking
its dead prey.

My heart drips with it
and my ears ring with it.
I have spoken of it
and written about it
and dreamt of it
and cried with it.
I have paced the floors
like a mad dog with it,
scratching the baseboards
of every wall
and sniffing each musty corner.

Longing for his scent
or a last message on scrap paper,
I have riffled through
suits and ties
like a stray mutt

begging for scraps.

In the end,
there was nothing.
Nothing but me.
Me and this grief.

Me and this grief
and a million places where
he should be.
A million things he should say.
A million things I wanted to say.
A million "Good byes"
left rattling in the wind
like aspen leaves in October.

The Gallery

After her husband died,
she surrounded herself with pictures.
The two of them on their wedding day,
big smiles and fresh flowers,
Sonja roses and baby's breath.
The two of them in Breckenridge,
loose jackets and restaurant cocktails.
The two of them in La Jolla,
gentle waves and sandy beaches.

She tended the photos
like treasured house plants,
dusting the glass,
talking to the smiling faces,
tenderly stroking the silver frames.

Her beloved dog, Nikki, followed her
from photo to photo,
room to room,
wagging her tail and
cocking her head
when her master spoke
to the reflective glass.

At dinner,
the quiet photos
waited in the background,
sharing her repast,
watching stiffly
from a distant reality.

At the end of the day,
she bid them all adieu,
dimming the lights and
pulling the curtains.

Though frozen moments in time,
she shared her life with them
and longed for a time of warmth
and a healing thaw.

Trying for a Perfect Day

Sometimes, when I feel
tears burning behind
my eyelids,

I shake my head
real hard and
fast, like

a cartoon character
whose whole body
gyrates in

a flurry of motion,
arms and legs
flailing and particles

flying off like
water droplets on
a wet dog.

Sometimes, when tears
leave my eyes and
roll down my hot face,

dripping onto my
blue jeans or
sometimes into

the white kitchen sink, if
I am standing there, watching
morning clouds,

they leave spots on
the denim or ricochet
onto the granite countertop,

making a perfect splash,
like the famous photo of
one drop of water.

Sometimes, if the tears
won't stop, I shake
my head real hard again,

rewinding the moment,
rolling the tears
back up

into my head, and
back into my brown eyes again, like

there never were any

denim spots or
perfect splashes or
any reason to ever cry.

In the End

In the end,
the sound of voices fade

away, like a long,
long train slowly

rounding the bend past
great corn fields and

thick-forested country roads and
white-shingled farm houses.

In the end,
tired eyes close, as if

in a dream, and
long arms stretch

out with reaching hands,
grasping and

picking at the sweet,

sweet air.

In the end,
strains of Bach and

Handel and
Mozart

fill the quiet room,
circling 'round and

'round, filling every crevice
with beauty and grace and

settling gently on
your soft hand

holding mine
forever.

Beth and Mike

Dr. Mike

"Captain" Mike

33

Honoring the Matriarchs

Grandma Standing

I am mesmerized by the picture
of my grandma, Maude, taken
the week of October 13th, 1958,
according to the Kodachrome ink stamp
on the back of the color photo.

She stands in the grassy back
yard of my childhood,
a small brown dog lying
contentedly at her feet.

Grandma smiles
with steady, be-speckled eyes,
the same sweet smile of
her daughter,
my mother.

Grandma's husband, Harry,
the railroad conductor,
died the year before,
after bidding everyone good night,
and all left the hospital
to go home for the night.

It was the first time
Grandma had envisioned a life
without Grandpa beside her
in their feather bed
on South 11th Street, but

a year later,
Grandma was standing alone
in our back yard
with an easy smile,
purse hanging from the crook
of her arm,
resolutely moving forward
without her conductor.

Mothers

Lately, I find myself
standing at the front door
looking through beveled glass to
"see what I can see,"

like my mother and
her mother
before mine.

Hands on their hips,
flowered aprons in place,
they looked.

Alice's laundry
on the line,
wooden clothespins
holding white cotton
sheets billowing
in the late summer breeze.

Mary tending her
flower garden,
kneeling with gloved hands,

almost in prayer,
beside her bright
yellow daisies and
red geraniums.

A lone brown squirrel
scampering
across the
tall telephone wire,
leaping from
wire to tree branch to
gray shingled roof.

In the kitchen,
warm sugar cookies baked
in deep ovens
while the mothers looked,
like this mother and
the mother after me.

The Fall

Her lovely eighty-five pounds
is engulfed by
the blue corduroy recliner
she brought with her
from Cartwright Drive,
the last sweet remnant of
her fifty-seven years
on the west side.

Now in the east-side
assisted living facility,
the shopping mall with
J.C. Penney's and Sear's
is just a stone's throw away,
a mockery of her
once-quick stride
and delight in
colorful clothing stores and
drugstore diners.

Her bruised arms cross over
her diminishing frame and
bony elbows press

into the soft sides
of her recliner
in rhythmic movement
as she works,
knit one, purl two,
carefully looping a strand of
variegated yarn
around her arthritic ninety-nine
year-old index finger,
making hash marks
in her side table spiral notebook
as a blue-green sweater
slowly emerges.

Dr. Lee told her
she would never walk
again after her last fall,
a broken left ankle.
To prove him wrong,
she has taken slow,
tentative steps again
with her rolling metal walker,
strolling the beige carpeted hallways of
Sterling House,
passing the rows of
closed apartment doors

concealing blaring televisions
and sleeping residents.

Twelve hundred miles away,
a brisk north wind
blows outside my kitchen window,
shaking the aspen leaves
clinging to their fading
summer green,
untold days away
from transition to
bright shimmering yellow.

Red Wagon

Mom often dozes
in her Indiana recliner while
goldfinch devour thistle
outside her window.

Tiny black claws grip
as the feed bag yields
to May breezes,
swinging methodically
on the branch
like the pendulum in
Grandma's Cottage Clock.

Pillows envelope Mom.
Two pillows under her.
One pillow behind her head and back.
One under each forearm and
under her bony ankles.

If she starts leaning in
her dreamless sleep,
sometimes pillows shift and
she is one

call light away from finally
meeting the one who calls
her name.

Eyes tightly closed in
my Colorado bed,
I imagine a comfortable Mom,
smiling and turning effortlessly
in her single bed,
happily stretching
every extremity of her tiny
99 year-old frame.

Two years ago,
Mom sat easily in
the velour-covered chair
she brought with her

from Cartwright Drive,
bringing her legs up
one by one,
drawing each knee
close to her chin.

While the Christmas clock
in her bedroom loudly marks

each second,
Mom slowly
counts the hours,
shifting uncomfortably
in her recliner,
looking at her watch,
looking out the window,
watching nameless passersby
roam the hall
with their walkers and canes.

No sweaty headband-covered runners
vie for the lead
in this race,
nor do any thoroughbreds
kick up dirt
rounding tight corners.

I clung to Mom's soft hand
as a child
while we walked briskly
down Peacock Road
to Cox's Supermarket.
My older brother, Tom,
followed us,
bringing the red wagon

for a walk he thought was
too long for his little sister.

Could someone please
bring the red wagon
for all of us now?

Grandma Maude

Grandma Maude

Mom

Where They Are

Was He Ever Here?

His presence sometimes seems
a distant memory.

That chair,
did he ever rest in it?

Were his warm hands ever
tightly grasped
around that doorknob?

Did he ever push that nail
with his worn hammer,
steel and brown and haunted
with his sweet muskiness?

Did his feet,
slow and heavy at day's end,
ever ascend those stairs,
aching for comfort,
longing for rest?

Did his weight ever
lay itself on that bed

53

and pull the sheet lightly over?

Was he ever really here?

Did he ever touch my mouth with his,
or tenderly caress my skin
with gentle hands,
soft and square and
full of strength?

Did he really share my life?

Did he really leave my side?

Was he ever really here?

Lying in Wait

Lying in wait,
he creeps into
the happiest of
my poems, like

the one about
selling my house and
looking forward to
the future and
new beginnings and
things like that.

Maybe it's because
his smiling picture rests
on the desk corner
near my laptop computer,

as though the
proximity of
his image
affects
the keys I strike or
the tenor of my words.

Or maybe it's because
the harder I try to
project a future
without him in it,

while sitting in his
black leather chair from
his college
administrative office

at the large wooden
computer desk
we bought together
in Colorado Springs,

the harder he tries to
impede my progress,

sending me to the kitchen
for more snacks
and a bottle of water or,

distracting me with
a bevy of gambel quail
scurrying outside
my office window.

Nikki lies on her
sheepskin dog bed,
legs long and limp,
eyes half-closed,
body twitching in a
canine dream,

oblivious to the
passage of time or
the difference between
me writing these words
and Mike.

When You Are Near

When you are near,
is it the quiet
rustling of leaves outside
my bedroom window,
or the faint shadow
seen from the corner
of my eye?

Is it my quick smile
when remembering an old joke, or
my childlike delight at
the tiniest insect
scurrying across
warm spring pavement?

When you are thinking
of me, is it the bright yellow
bird at the birdfeeder or
a white passing cloud,
slowly drifting out of sight?

When you come to me
in dreams, is that

an answered question,
or are these words written
by you, as you hover
peacefully over the back
of my desk chair,
softly guiding my fingers
across the page?

I Am Not Remembering

Even though this Thursday is October 18th,
the 26th anniversary of our wedding,
I am not remembering it. I am tired of acknowledging
all these anniversaries and
birthdays and special days that roll by,

year after year, month after month
without even as much as a card
from Mike, or Mom and Dad, or
Aunt Mary and Uncle Dan and Uncle Clay,
or Grandma and Grandpa,
or all the rest of them,
who are apparently
quite content where they are,

leaving me to fend for myself
here on earth,
stuck with gravity and
cold winter days and
insurance bills, while they rest on

floating white clouds,
fanning themselves with huge green palm leaves,

white-robed angels feeding them
sweet peeled grapes or
shuffling their favorite deck of Texaco cards
for the perfect Euchre game in heaven,

or wherever it is all these dead people go,
all MY dead people,
after they
close their eyes and sigh
that last sigh, wilting softly
like deflated balloons.

No, I am not remembering
Mike's 60th birthday or
the sixth anniversary of
the day he died, nor am I remembering

Mom's 102nd birthday or Grandma's 130th,
or Dad's 100th. Who could possibly imagine
my sweet dad any older than he was at age 57,
the day he died in 1969?

No, I am not remembering
the anniversaries of my dead people
anymore.

They can mock me with
their smiling faces
from the still photos on the bookshelf, or
taunt me with moving classical guitar melodies, or
beautiful darting goldfinches
in the spring, or the rich aroma of
freshly-baked white bread
on Saturday mornings, but
I am not remembering them anymore.

Where They Are

When I tuck the sheets
tightly around the mattress corners,
smoothing out
invisible wrinkles,
pulling the quilted bedspread
evenly over the sides,

Mom is there,
smiling her approval,
sighing deeply and
reaching forward with
long, graceful fingers.

During animated political
conversations and
giggly, rough and tumble
games with the grandkids,

Paul is there, laughing,
tickling, egging them on
in his bright red cardigan
and Harry Cary glasses.

During prayer at the noisy
family-filled dinner table,

Helen is there
with a nervous smile,
honoring her God,
relishing her loved ones and
fretting about imperfect
side dishes or
mis-matched dinnerware.

Strolling beautiful
department stores
lingering over fine clothing,
or quietly studying and
giggling during
complicated card games,

Aunt Mary is there,
arms gently crossed,
ever-ponderous,
peeking over Mom's shoulder,
loving the game.

When I solve the problem after
hours of thoughtful

work and calculation,
or stand quietly
in the background
observing the noisy group,
longing for peace and
social comfort,
or when I fly confidently
in the smallest of airplanes,

Mike is there,
smiling, imagining,
hoping, loving.

Paul and Helen

Uncle Dan and
Aunt Mary

Mom, Beth, and Dad

Life Equals Transition

The Border

When we headed out
the front door
late Tuesday afternoon,
just around the bend,
beyond the yapping Pomeranian and
the rental house with mulch
for a front yard,

a May storm was brewing,
shaking tree branches and
pushing rumbling thunder up
against our backs.

Despite the leisurely walk
I had promised,
we were suddenly hurrying
down the street,
me, making quick glances
over my shoulder at
the darkening sky,
Nikki, straining at her leash,
reaching around the mailbox for
one more sniff.

Halfway before we arrived
at our front door,
Nikki was panting
in the 60-degree weather,
trying to keep my pace, but
slowing
as I quickened.

After snacks and supper,
she eased herself onto the
soft orthopedic dog bed,
scratching at the sheepskin,
working to fluff the material to
suit her aging body.

Later, tossing and turning
in my own bed,
visions of my failing mom
drifted behind my closed eyes as

Nikki slept,
her slow, deep respirations
like those of so many
tip-toeing between
this side and
the other.

Someone New

We moved the stuff
out of Aunt Mary's attic today.
Boxes of books and black and white
photographs of aunts and uncles
no one remembers.

She is giving us the antiques
but selling the rest.
We gather around the piles,
whispering in small groups
like mourners at a funeral parlor.

After we loaded everything
into the U-Haul,
Mike and I walked around the yard
one last time.

I showed him where we used to plant corn,
where the dog run used to be,
and where our family used to sit
under the shade tree on those
unbearably hot Sunday afternoons.

Aunt Mary says that she and Clay
have set a date for the movers,
so it's certain they will be married
by then.

Aunt Mary's first husband, Dan,
used to get so mad at Aunt Mary
when she won playing cards,
but after 50 years of marriage,
he loved her more than anyone could.

I think he'd be happy
she found someone new.
I just wish I knew
for sure.

What I Know

There is the kind of learning
that comes
from working hard
to ready your house
for public view and
having only one person
come to see it,
your curious neighbor
from two doors down.

And the kind of learning
that comes
from returning
to your home
and discovering that
your garage door
will only go
part-way up
and you have to
leave your Buick
parked in the driveway
on this very windy
April day,

collecting tumbleweeds,
layers of dust and
curious stares.

And the kind of learning
that comes
from understanding that
your replacement debit card
for the one that fell
out of your pants pocket yesterday
at the local thrift store
won't arrive until
late afternoon,
four days from now.

This learning is different
from the kind that comes
from the realization that
after almost five years
alone,
you still feel
married to the man
who promised his life to you
in October of 1986,
sweetly reciting his marital vows
and messages of hope,

but instead,

suddenly left you alone
in the summer of 2006,
when he crashed his
little plane –
the plane you didn't want him
to buy –
into a mountainside
of the beautiful Colorado Rockies.

This kind of learning
is the kind that comes
from the deep knowing that
even though
no one came to see your house,
it will sell.

Even though you lost your debit card,
you will get a new one.

Even though the garage door is broken,
it will be fixed.

Even though your husband died,

you didn't.

The Buyers

Sitting in the warm spring sun
on my oak deck
this bright Cinco de Mayo,

I am wondering if
the people who buy
my house
will drive a two-tone Subaru
like the one that got
Marjorie and Hector
and me

up that rugged
Colorado mountainside
the year after Mike died,
straining and lurching
its way
until we finally

reached our summit and
sat with binoculars
in plastic lawn chairs,
staring at the

lush green mountain
before us

while small white butterflies
flitted around our ankles
in the tall mountain grass,
enjoying the late summer
lavender and
yellow wildflowers.

Or if they will drive a
burgundy Buick,
like the one
Mom drove
for years,
delivering Meals on Wheels
in her small
Midwestern town until
she was 92 years old,
and too frail to lift
her silver walker
with the cloth bag attached,
into and out of
the trunk.

But mostly, I am

wondering how to
drive this tan Buick –

the one that
belonged to Mike,

the one that he bought
in exchange for the
white Park Avenue
to appease me and
save a little money,

the one that he left
in the garage
and to which he
never returned –

away from this house
that we built together
with hopes
for the future,

and that I filled with
memories and
pictures of Mike and
Mom and Aunt Mary, and

Helen and Paul, and
grandparents and
all the dead I know, but

postponed planning
for a life
without them.

Precipice

She tip-toed gently to the edge,
peering over slowly,
sweaty hands clasped together,
fingers intertwined,
as if in prayer.

Steadying her feet
in the loose soil,
she kicked away stones,
rounding out foot holds
with her heel.

Leaning her head back,
she gazed to the heavens as
an eagle soared
over the terra firma,
swooping in wide, quiet patterns,
outlining the canyon,
re-designing the sky
with its outstretched wings.

Slowly, she unlaced her fingers,
red with fear and pain, and

lifted her weary arms
to the cloudless blue above,
reaching toward the light,
reaching toward the beauty,
reaching toward the hope for strength and a
clarity of vision.

Aunt Mary and
Uncle Clay

Grandma and Grandpa, Mom and
Aunt Mary

Rituals

Luciana

Early July mornings, she crouches down
in the green of her front lawn,
white broad-brimmed hat shading her
smiling face, garden-gloved-hands working
through the blades, pulling up
dandelions and other nameless weeds.

Her husband, Sherman, watches
from the kitchen, pulling the newspaper
close as he sips hot coffee, sometimes
swirling a teaspoon through
the dark liquid, gently
clinking the insides of the Italian china with
her family's silver from the old country.

Pulling back the window sheers, he smiles,
admiring the slow curve of her hips and
the red waves of hair falling loosely
about her narrow shoulders. Closing
his eyes, he twists the smooth gold
wedding band slowly around
his small third finger.

Days after his car was broadsided
on a bright Saturday afternoon,
she wept with their children, slowly passing

his ring between them, each rubbing it sweetly
with thumb and forefinger,
gazing at the impossible glint from
the brilliant summer sun.

Back in the yard, white clouds drift slowly
overhead and she closes her eyes,
gray hair cascading from
under her garden hat as she
leans her head back, basking in
the sun's warmth and memories
of Sherman, peering out at her
through soft window sheers,
as gentle as the clouds above.

At a Funeral

My bereaved white-haired friend sits
in the front church pew
flanked by her loving daughters.
They are tightly wound
together with jacketed arms
and long scarves and
a loving history of
shared losses.

No one breathes as
their dear friend
from England reads
their words,
reads the truest feelings
the family could not speak
aloud,
for fear of
crumbling
down.

Do the gray-haired mourners
wonder if
they will be next,

shifting restlessly in
the wooden pews,
staring at the red Methodist hymnals
through round glasses and
silently brushing their
black wool pants?

The minister gave assurances of
God's promised heaven
to the tearful bereaved and
the frowning doubters.

After the last hymn,
the dark-haired man
next to me
closed his eyes,
silently reaching for his
brown tweed coat,
slowly slipping his arms
into the lined sleeves
one by one,
defying the cold and
an uncertain forecast.

Another Day

There is something especially troubling
about healthcare
workers who smoke.

Stethoscope hanging
from their necks,
they sit
alone on the curb, or
in small clusters on a bench
across from the hospital,

gazing at the white haze
drifting from their long cigarettes while
chemotherapy and radiation patients
drive quietly by,

gazes averted, heading to
their cancer
treatment appointments.

It's like the workers
don't get it, or that they plot
ways to sabotage

the patients, already
confused by their fate.

In spite of
all the lessons
in school and
all the words of
their parents and
all the warnings
on the pack and
in the news,

they succumb to
this life-sucking vice while
caring for many of those who would,
on any given day,
close their eyes in gratitude
for just one more
deep, long quiet breath.

Fowl Mourning

The ducks are in mourning,
waddling single file,
silently, solemnly
to the lakeside tragedy.

Heads lowered in respect
they pass quietly,
acknowledging their dead family
lying mangled and stiff
among the rocks.

On a nearby dock,
we lie sunbathing,
stroking our bodies with lotion
in a mystic ritual of self-worship,
oblivious to the funeral
and the passage of our lives.

It's All About Love

Like a Bird

In deep, quiet sleep,
I softly reach for space,
stretching to feel your warmth,
aching to hear your breath,
deep and slow and
heavily life-filled.

The unrelenting calendars have
brought me to this moment, and
I press full-body against it,
calling your name and
straining to pull you with me
from yesterday.

The memories that unite us
unravel like a frayed rope, and
I tumble backwards,
searching for footing,
grasping wildly at the air.

Regaining my focus,
you are suspended in the clouds,
smiling and waving and calling,

"I love you!"

"Come back! Come back!"
I am running and waving.

Untethered, you float,
gently reaching for the sun,
smiling and waving
as you slowly ascend.

Like a bird,
you are gone from my sight.
I am still running and calling,
"Come back! Come back! I love you!"

In the deepening violet of dusk,
I close my eyes to the stillness
and breathe in your depth,
lulled to sleep by
the gentle breezes in the trees, whispering,
"I am always with you."

My Heart Will Stay

In 1985, when we met
on a cold February evening,
you held the umbrella
high overhead as we
dashed to the Chevy you borrowed
from your parents.

Before the play,
we shared stories of photographing
the flooding Wabash River and
relishing long walks
in the Willow Street cemetery.

On our third date,
the social work banquet
where you won the award,
you offered me
a stick of Wrigley's
to calm my nerves, and
took a stick for yourself,
so I wouldn't be nervous
alone.

After all the sweet walks and
late nights and long talks and
long after the wedding and
Chris' graduation and after
all the administrative jobs in
Vincennes and in Pueblo,

in August of 2006,
while I was in Indiana
visiting my mom,
you packed up your little plane,
that sweet little red and white
1958 Piper Comanche,
and with a smile,
launched yourself
into the sky,
headed for Durango,
headed for glory.

Twenty-seven years
after that cold February evening,
I buried you across the road
from your parents on a
cool September afternoon.

It could have been the spot

where we walked our beagle,
Kizzy, in 1985,
throwing sticks across the lush green lawn,
running and laughing,
cupping water from the cemetery faucet
in our hands for her to drink.

I only know that
wherever it was,
wherever you are.
my heart will always stay.

Gratitude

As golden dog hair grays
around her soulful brown eyes and
sweet muzzle, it is sometimes
debatable if that second walk
through the quiet neighborhood is
possible, or even appropriate, as
Nikki pants from fatigue and
tender arthritic joints.

But sometimes,
on warm spring evenings,
as the orange sun sets
behind tall aspens and
distant rooftops,
we venture
out of the cul-de-sac,

rounding the curve and
slowly making our way
past yellow stucco patio homes and
meticulously planted young pines,
filled with the bright song of
goldfinches and

house sparrows darting
between dry limbs.

Nikki pauses every few yards,
staring ahead, seemingly
assessing her ability to
make the distance, or
when interested,
investigating a lawn,
pushing tender grass aside
with her snout,
reading reports of
earlier visitors.

Weary and satisfied
after the short walk,
we lumber home,
Nikki with her
gimpy right leg,
me with my left, grateful for
one more journey together.

Nikki's Dreams

My sweet old dog, Nikki,
stands quietly
at the front door,
watching with
steady brown eyes
through the side glass panel as
my tan Buick
backs down the
short driveway and
heads down the
north side street,

away from
our warm stucco home,
the orthopedic dog beds and
the 20-pound bag of
Purina Dog Food
for Seniors
tucked away
in the two-car garage.

While I stop at the
corner Walgreen's for
greeting cards and a

gallon of skim milk,
Nikki reluctantly returns
to her large cushion,
sighing heavily while
she waits,
easing her tired body onto
the thick sheepskin and
rounding herself gently
into a sweet arc
in front of the fireplace.

Minutes later, I
tip-toe onto the cold entry-way tile.
Nikki is snoring deeply, but
raises her head,
glancing at me with
grateful sleepy eyes.

Tomorrow, we shall
walk the street of
Nikki's dreams.

Bliss

She sleeps quietly
in my darkened bedroom
on the extra-thick,
sheepskin-covered mattress
I bought her
at PetSmart last week.

So still,
I strain to watch
her belly rise and fall .

The extra-long walk
at Elizabeth Street Park
tuckered her out.

She doesn't flinch
as a stack of books
on the end table by the couch
fall to the floor.

Earlier this month,
I debated about a new dog bed
for my old dog.

But now, as I watch her
lying contentedly limp
on her extra-comfortable bed,

I know that
if she lives but
one more second,

the new dog bed
is worth it
for my old dog to experience
this kind of bliss,
and for me to love her.

Nikki, The Best
Dog Ever
Created!

Now and Forever

Ovation

Dropping my right arm
to my side,
violin bow still in hand,
I slowly turn my head from
side to side, relaxing
tense neck and shoulder muscles,
breathing deeply after
beautiful Vivaldi, when

the quiet row of
framed family photos
on the bookshelf nearby
catches my eye, an audience of
dead people
in permanent stances,
smiling their approval with
silent applause and
imperceptible head nods.

Surely there could be
no higher praise.

Sentry

A poem for my grandsons,
the blood of the blood of
my husband, long gone
in time, but ever-present
in three young boys

spread across
the Midwest like
smooth peanut butter
on warm wheat toast.

Gathering in
small groups on hot
summer days, reaching
tattered basketball nets
with long arms,
they run,

dripping sweat from
their brown waves
over the eyes of
their grandfather,

whose life courses
through their young veins.

At day's end,
they rest,
shading their faces
from the late
afternoon sun,
looking past

their long, dark shadows
towards the next day, as

tall ash and cottonwood
stand quietly at their side,
a sentry in time.

A Time for Love

Got a Christmas card from
one of the college presidents
with whom Mike was good friends, Linda,
before he left his college,
and me,
and this planet,
in August of 2006.

Staring at Linda's name
and her Christmas family photo,
it was as though no time,
and all time,
had passed.

Mike was back at the kitchen table
on Tierra Casa Drive,
reading the morning paper,
eating his warm oatmeal.

I was standing behind his breakfast chair
in my pajamas,
arms draped around his chest,
kissing his warm neck,

pulling his soft cheek close to mine.

At once,
I was alone,
in this new house,
on this new street,
on the other side of town,
in December of 2012.

Fluttering my eyelids lightly,
it was 2006, and
Mike was there again at the table,
with the oatmeal,
with my arms draped around him.

Before Mike died,
I laid in the crook of his left arm,
drifting off to sleep
while he read his aviation magazines
in the dimly lit bedroom,
studying navigation rules and
dreaming of bright, shiny, new planes.

Opening my eyes again
in the new house,
on the new street,

Mike stands behind my breakfast chair,
arms draped around my shoulders,
pulling my soft cheek
close to his.

Finding Direction

Drove through the old neighborhood
this cold January evening
four months after
the move.

Took a good
fifteen minutes to get there
from my new
quiet neighborhood on
the north side of town.

My car seemed confused
by the return route,
bucking against the
frequent pot holes
and slowing in front of
the impatient Ford sedan
confident of
its destination.

But when we got there,
up the hill it went,
past the lit subdivision sign and

around the curve to
Tierra Casa Drive.

I don't remember the sky
being this velvety dark or
the white stars
sparkling so brightly over
my old neighbors.

Nancy's house was first,
with her sweet little
three year-old, Elise, and their
beautiful back yard pool, then

around the bend was
Carla and Joe and

half their family who
shared the large home
after Joe filed
for disability.

Next to them was
my old place.

My car crept by

the darkened house,
seemingly fearful
of the life-sized garden figurines
in the yard,
silhouetted against the
stucco exterior
by the bright moonlight.

No hand-carved
"Welcome" bear from Westcliffe
graced the front porch, nor did any
sweet old dog
peer through the
side glass panel of
the front door.

The basketball goal,
whose pole Mike finally had
cemented into the ground,
was still standing, though,
towering over the driveway as
a permanent marker of
our beautiful lives there.

Easing out of the subdivision,
careful of the mule deer who

frequented the entryway,
my car slowly gathered speed and
confidently headed due north
to Paseo Del Tesoro Street,
as sure as any compass.

Hidden Change

Waiting in my idling car
at the Taco Bell drive-through,
my fingers sifted through
a handful of copper
pennies saved
in the pocket of
the driver's side door.

Grasping each penny
between thumb
and forefinger,
the imprinted date
came into focus and I
closed my eyes,
gently recalling each year.

1980: A new university graduate,
college clothes on wire hangers and
wooden crates of LP's
pressed against the windows of
my two-door, 1966 Chrysler Newport,

I drove down

unfamiliar, two-lane Indiana roads
towards the small, rural town of
my first real job,

weeping as I left
my first love behind, but
smiling broadly in anticipation of
a new life.

2010: My beautiful, amazing Mom whispered,
"Good-bye,"
on July First,
at the frail age of 99,
unable to stay

long enough to celebrate
her 100th birthday with
her devoted
Beta Sigma Phi sisters or
clasp her loving daughter's hand
one last time before
she left this earth.

My sweet Aunt Mary
slipped away ten weeks later,
softly calling to her

older sister as they
skipped hand-in-hand down
a beautiful invisible path.

1976: Richmond High School graduation.
Bags packed with confidence and pride,
the entire family, except for
my older brother, Tom,
who couldn't leave
his park ranger job,

filled Uncle Dan's
old station wagon
like the "Beverly Hillbillies," and
headed to Indiana University,
hauling boxes and bags
into and out of
the tall university dorm.

As my family slowly drove away from
the dorm entrance,
my head turned,
brushing a sleeve
against my face,
wiping away big, rolling tears before
joining the other freshmen, hiding

their damp eyes, busily
studying campus maps.

2012: The breast cancer year.
This penny, so
shiny and unmarred seemed a
symbol of hope and
new beginnings, as I

caressed it,
slowly turning the coin from
tail side to head side and
back again,
as though
my fate could be determined
by the flipping of it.

As the restaurant speaker blared,
I pulled ahead,
counting out the change and
pressing the final penny down
onto the metal counter,
head's up.

I Am From

I am from
the Midwest,
with tall golden corn stalks
and lush green
fields of melons
and soybeans,
acres of Sunday dinners.

I am from
Helen and Cliff,
who loved me like
their seed,
holding me tight
with long, strong arms,
plucking me
from foster care
like a farmer
choosing a ripe, sweet apple.

I am from
flour-coated kitchen counters and
a smiling, aproned mother,
Saturday morning
apple pies and

fork-pressed peanut butter
cookies, made with
real butter.

I am from
a white T-shirt-clad father
quietly
doing Army sit-ups
before his 5:00 daily
trek to Perfect Circle factory,
metal lunch box
in hand and warm
thermos under arm,

smiling as he watched
his little girl
skip up the ramp behind him
to the factory door.

I am from
cold winter mornings
standing on the
kitchen furnace vent
eating white Wonder Bread,
giggling while
my pink flannel gown from

Montgomery Ward's
billowed around me
like Barbie's prom dress
in my Barbie Dream House.

I am from
crisp Sunday
dresses and white patent
leather shoes from Sears,
and a quarter for Sunday School
at the First Christian Church.

I am from
hopscotch and
jump rope and Hula Hoop
and four square and red rover.

I am from
tender beef pot roast and
warm carrots and potatoes and slow
Sunday afternoon family drives
on the country roads of
Wayne County
in the blue, four-door Dodge
with radio knob letters
that spelled,

"D-O-D-G-E."

I am from
regular trips on my
big brother's shoulders
to Carne's Soda Bar and
small paper bags of
candy necklaces, cinnamon Teddy Bears and
Giant Sweet Tarts.

I am from
love
forever
and forever
family,
and am forever linked to
those resting
deep
under the green,
green earth of
Earlham Cemetery.

Mom, Dad, Tom, Beth

Mike's Son, Beth's Stepson, Chris

Grandsons: Chase, Nolan, and Gavin

About the Author:

Beth Bricker Davis has been a lifelong writer and has found great solace using the written word as an emotional outlet. She has worked in the social work field for more than thirty years, the last eight and a half years as a hospice counselor. She lives in Pueblo, Colorado, to where she moved in 2000, from her home state of Indiana.